D1557948

Creepy Crawlies
Black Widow Spiders

by Megan Borgert-Spaniol

BLASTOFF! READERS

BELLWETHER MEDIA • MINNEAPOLIS, MN

Note to Librarians, Teachers, and Parents:

Blastoff! Readers are carefully developed by literacy experts and combine standards-based content with developmentally appropriate text.

Level 1 provides the most support through repetition of high-frequency words, light text, predictable sentence patterns, and strong visual support.

Level 2 offers early readers a bit more challenge through varied simple sentences, increased text load, and less repetition of high-frequency words.

Level 3 advances early-fluent readers toward fluency through increased text and concept load, less reliance on visuals, longer sentences, and more literary language.

Level 4 builds reading stamina by providing more text per page, increased use of punctuation, greater variation in sentence patterns, and increasingly challenging vocabulary.

Level 5 encourages children to move from "learning to read" to "reading to learn" by providing even more text, varied writing styles, and less familiar topics.

Whichever book is right for your reader, Blastoff! Readers are the perfect books to build confidence and encourage a love of reading that will last a lifetime!

This edition first published in 2016 by Bellwether Media, Inc.

No part of this publication may be reproduced in whole or in part without written permission of the publisher. For information regarding permission, write to Bellwether Media, Inc., Attention: Permissions Department, 5357 Penn Avenue South, Minneapolis, MN 55419.

Library of Congress Cataloging-in-Publication Data

Borgert-Spaniol, Megan, 1989-
  Black Widow Spiders / by Megan Borgert-Spaniol.
    pages cm. – (Blastoff! readers. Creepy Crawlies)
  Summary: "Developed by literacy experts for students in kindergarten through grade three, this book introduces black widow spiders to young readers through leveled text and related photos"– Provided by publisher.
  Audience: Ages 5-8.
  Audience: K to grade 3.
  Includes bibliographical references and index.
  ISBN 978-1-62617-299-9 (hardcover : alk. paper)
  1. Black widow spider–Juvenile literature. I. Title.
  QL458.42.T54B67 2016
  595.4'4–dc23
                        2015028690

Printed in the United States of America, North Mankato, MN.

Table of Contents

Warning Marks

Black widow spiders are **arachnids** with a mean bite.

They have marks that warn of **venom**. Males are small with red and white marks.

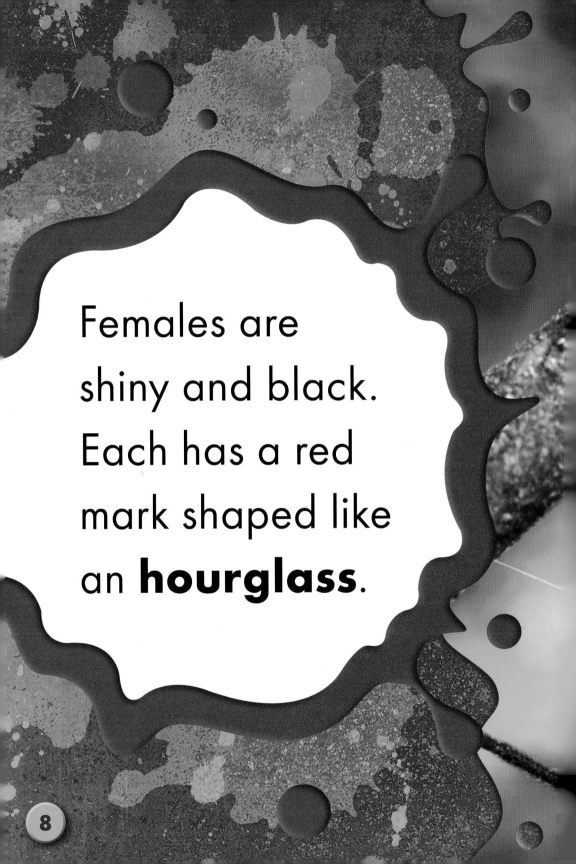

Females are shiny and black. Each has a red mark shaped like an **hourglass**.

Building Webs

Black widow spiders hide in dark places. They build webs near the ground.

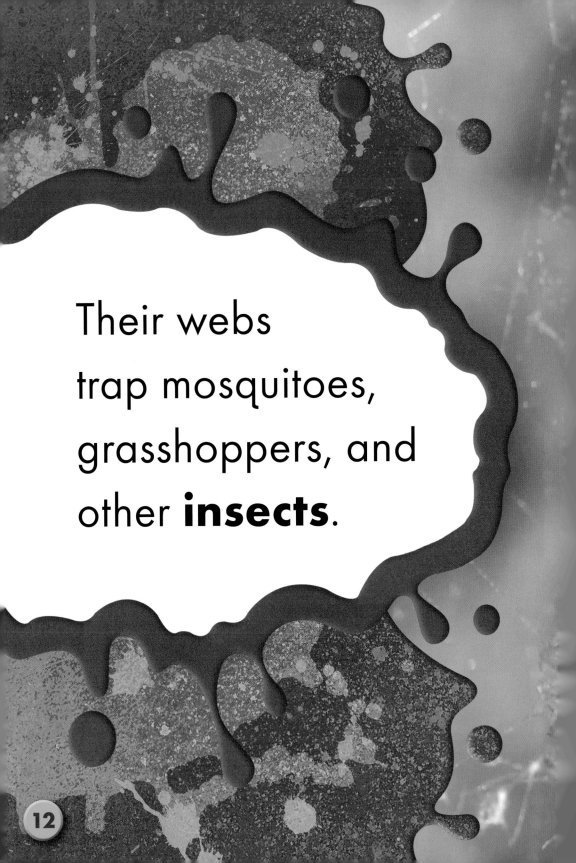

Their webs
trap mosquitoes,
grasshoppers, and
other **insects**.

Fangs and Venom

These spiders wrap their **prey** in **silk**. They bite the prey with their **fangs**.

Venom flows
from the fangs.
Black widow
venom makes big
animals sick!

Spiderlings

Females lay hundreds of eggs. They keep them safe with silk.

eggs in silk

Spiderlings break out of the eggs. Then they **balloon** to a new home!

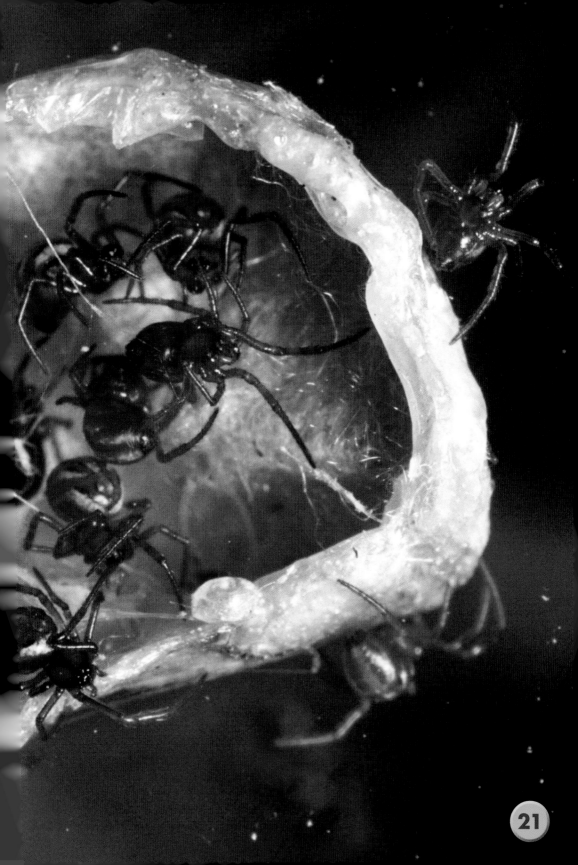

21

Glossary

arachnids—small animals with eight legs; an arachnid's body is divided into two parts.

balloon—to be carried by the wind to a new location

fangs—sharp teeth; venom often flows through fangs.

hourglass—an object that measures time; an hourglass has wide ends and a skinny middle.

insects—small animals with six legs and hard outer bodies; an insect's body is divided into three parts.

prey—animals that are hunted by other animals for food

silk—a strong, soft material

spiderlings—young spiders

venom—a poison

To Learn More

AT THE LIBRARY

Borgert-Spaniol, Megan. *Spiders*.
Minneapolis, Minn.: Bellwether Media, 2015.

Kolpin, Molly. *Black Widow Spiders*.
Mankato, Minn.: Capstone Press, 2011.

Marsh, Laura F. *Spiders*. Washington, D.C.:
National Geographic, 2011.

ON THE WEB

Learning more about
black widow spiders is
as easy as 1, 2, 3.

1. Go to www.factsurfer.com.

2. Enter "black widow spiders" into the
   search box.

3. Click the "Surf" button and you will see a
   list of related web sites.

With factsurfer.com, finding more information
is just a click away.

Index